Today is the First of April 2018!

I am so Thankfully Grateful and Blessed to Repent and Surrender to the Forgiveness that is Life itself!

Writing Poetry and Self-Publishing my very own style of books has become a very huge part of my life and self-healing process because I am always in the process of being open and learning from the work I am given!

My name is Lavinia De Ayr and I
write under the Pen Name and
Personal Mantra

Natural Flowism

A Freedom of Being!

I uploaded my latest book to Kdp Amazon Yesterday called

THE HATRED

Abused yet The Cursed One!

Not writing to many details for the description other than to mention it was a collection of Poems

Woke up this morning and decided to re-write the description and then became complete inspired to have one of my typical throw down question session about stalking!

Finding myself asking who so ever the reader would be if they could take the quiz of rhetorical questions. Having finished I thought it would be a great idea to

make those questions into another
one of my pamphlet style of books!

The QUIZ BITE

Introduction

Questioning everything that is ~ forms a big part of the effect of being stalked by someone!

Are you willing to take the quizzes set out below?

If you have not been stalked are willing to find out how much you know?

Read my Self-Healing Books

Look at the art collections

Can you decipher what went on?

www.naturalflowism.com

https://www.saatchiart.com/art-collection/Painting-Photography/Buy-a-Story-Board/389344/188557/view

https://www.saatchiart.com/art-collection/Painting/STALKING-MOST-SCATHING-FLASHBACK-WORK/389344/195323/view

https://www.saatchiart.com/art-collection/Drawing/Annex-of-Visual-Intimidation/389344/225551/view https://www.saatchiart.com/art-collection/Drawing-Collage-Painting/THE-CAST/389344/226511/view

How conceptual are the events being created toward you, and around you?

Is there such a thing as 'too much' consciousness especially if your life, your private life is being threatened?

Who in society allows individuals to act anonymously? (this affects not everybody knows who their stalker is!)

What happens if you are poor, working class, and are stalked by some who is rich, filthy rich, or filthy, and rich?

How much crime does that allow?

What about when it is female stalking female black stalking black who is going to believe that?

When a cult is formed who regulates them as non-poisonous?

Are you aware of the energetic practices of today's cults?

Are you aware of the dangerous hypnotic practices BY THOSE WHO CLAIM OTHERS ARE CURSED?

Or of the misuse of projecting negative energy in the same

distant healers use to do good and heal others?

If others say what is happening is nothing to do with you ~ why is it others can still get to you?

Be outside you work place?

Where you shop ~ Every time you go into a shop anywhere regardless without advising you will be there?

Are you wrong to you observe yourself constantly being observed?

Who observes?

How much awareness would a stranger have about what an individual goes through faced with a campaign of morbid jealously?

How much work will have to be done to ensure someone's life and efforts always goes wrong?

Can you calculate how many witnesses will be made along the way?

Can you figure out after curating so many witness how a stalker can remain anonymous and still get away?

Was I - who is being stalked wrong to ask why?

Can you see through to where there are lies?

What lies am i - who is stalked telling myself?

Who has the right to legally blame
and shame without taking
available appropriate action?

Employment?

Deployment?

What right does an individual
have to be informed when someone
clearly sets out to destroy and tear
their life apart?

Would know if someone's
employer was abusing their power
as an employer and stepping over
the mark of their personal
boundaries into the private life of a
current or ex-employee?

When someone cannot leave you
alone and goes as far to keep up a
pattern of intimidation hoaxing

using the emergency services –
what are the broader implications
of such an allowance of careful
planning?

Is the nitty gritty of such a situation
just for fun or a real distraction and
cover up of a style of murder?

Who or what will keep up the idea
that an individual shall never be
good for anything else but to be a
modern-day slave in service but in
the most derogatory and abusive
way?

Would you automatically think
someone who is challenges with
writing correctly does not deserve
to pay attention too?

Will ignoring someone with a spelling or grammar failure put their life in further danger?

If someone wrote to you for help but the report or letter they wrote was littered with mistakes but not enough to not be understood would you still be a snob and ignore that person?

If someone started to mention to you, they were being stalked by someone else will you immediately shut them down?

If the answer is yes – why?

Would you automatically think if a woman is being stalked by a man she should just surrender to him?

If your answer is automatically yes!

Would it ever occur to you that she may have been pursued since childhood?

Be it male telling a female he had been stalked, or vice e versa would it ever occur to that what they are describing may be from an unprosecuted violent crime?

Would you continue believe what appears and is perceived as just a mild nuisance of anti-social behaviour which has been consistently reported over many years to be just as it appears, or will you keep an open mind to their being other dangers, or an escalation toward danger?

Could you tell the difference between someone affected by

being stalked by someone else, and the actual perpetrator of stalking behaviours?

Who would you side with in a campaign of grooming?

You are approached by someone ever so gentle claiming they miss their best friend they seem genuine because if they are ill with jealously they are, they ask you to let them know wherever, and whenever you see them. What would you do?

Are you aware that stalking behaviours are not just akin to strangers, ex dates, partners, husbands and wives?

Are you aware that members from the same family, and even church members can also suffer from stalking behaviours?

It is extremely difficult when people leave a family, or group setting suddenly.

What can further appear to blur the boundaries lines is a need for diplomacy.

During an abusive upbringing as a child of the family at a dependant age. You are forced to continue to blend, and get along with everyone despite having been raped, and violently beaten, with other add ons of ongoing emotional, spiritual, violent torture. Which may last years after separation.

People who are well educated about abuse would recognise and understand not to take for granted the need for separation and estrangement. However, where incest and other violence's are thought of as acceptable and even normal. Estrangement is not understood and taken for granted as not needed! As a result, despite the perpetration of rape and violence one who leaves to be free may still be pursued by those who do not see violence as a need to break a family apart. It can be an incredibly complex dilemma. The need to be loyal. The need to fully repair. The need and ability to fully break free to access the ability to understand how to heal!

The complete misunderstanding of those within a Family or Church Group who then organise all day spies, and covert investigations as you try and pull your life together from their wickedness, and rape!

Do you understand what it feels like to never be able to be allowed to break free?

The ferocity and intensity of someone's else's need to pin down your whereabouts?

What you do if your neighbour started leaving a trail of evidence which proves they know where you have been?

Would you try and reconcile with them?

Or would you realise you are facing danger?

What you do if that neighbour continues to be friendly yet dismisses any conversation about their nosey behaviour?

What would you do if you realised you were being followed to and from work by your neighbours?

What do you think of people in general who you always see by themselves - alone?

Do you often assume they are weird and unfriendly?

Do you automatically assume they are needy and vulnerable?

Do you ever think is that person being attacked by somebody?

Or is being deliberately isolated?

If you were told by someone in that person's family that the person who is always seen alone is not to be treated fairly or nicely would you just go along with what you are told?

Would question if there was a history of a variety of violence, incest, or pure cruelty?

As a woman would you recognise a man who has been battered?

As a woman do you agree a man should automatically be left with nothing if he fails to want to be in a relationship with a woman, or the mother of his children?

Which way would you turn if you found yourself under attack because you do not want to have a same sex relationship?

How would you deal with someone who got to the point of stalking you because they because they became convinced you were single because you wanted to change your gender choice?

Would this be motive enough for murder?

Would you automatically presume a woman innocent of sexual misconduct?

As a man are you aware of the sexual advances of women on women?

Have you ever thought about how hard it can be to return to the dating scene after rape, incest, violence, stalking?

Would you recognise it in someone?

How sensitive would be toward someone who has been ripped off – let down – disbelieved?

Are you willing to spend a minute or a second to decipher why a person would choose to share their experience of being stalked over and over again?

Can you figure out why a person can be stalked, and nobody be willing to tell them the truth of who and why?

If somebody of great fame, fortune, heritance, and stature was known to stalk those less cable of defending themselves would you have the back bone to approach them and tell them?

Or would you continue to enjoy the suspense?

Is really uncommon to not want to relive what was a reasonable, or very unhappy school daze?

Would you recognise the bravado of one who is too scared to be alone claiming the person they are stalking actually needs them?

These are just a sample of many other serious questions which ought to be asked about stalking in general.

But not only in general. When children who are abused do they have a chance to ever really be free?

To be honest had I not been stalked I may have never asked any of this!

I am no a 53-year-old woman and going through the experience of stalking despite having years when I almost felt detached and disconnected enough the experience of being stalked dragged right back in it all again!

I always believe despite being the writer of works and the asker of many questions. I am probably the one with the most to learn.

Simply because I get so deeply engrossed in the work~ it is not always possible to be objective enough!

Many would not spare the time needed to even ask, and hopefully one day I would never feel the constant need to ask or give rise to those who enjoy the control they have gained in the knowledge they have attained due to the secrets they use to plague!

Natural Flowism

A

Freedom

Of

Being!

Let Freedom Reign!

I give continued to Thanks to my family who continue to give me the space I need to fully repair and heal!

Amen!

May you all be continually blessed if you so choose to receive the blessing!

Selah!

A Freedom of Being!

Created in and Inspired by Life in London, England

**All
Rights
Reserved
2018**

I am so Thankfully, Grateful, and Blessed to ask, Repent and Surrender to the Forgiveness Life is!

Amen!

www.ingramcontent.com/pod-product-compliance
Lightning Source LLC
Chambersburg PA
CBHW070955220526
45471CB00007B/3042